MEETING MASTERY:

A LEAD ON TO BETTER CONVERSATIONS & DECISIONS

BY BRENDA DIXON

Table of Content

Mastering Meetings: A Leadership Journey

Introduction: Why Meetings Matter

Meetings are the heartbeat of any organization. They are where ideas are born, decisions are made, and connections are strengthened. Yet, for many leaders and teams, meetings often feel like a drain on time and energy—a necessary but unproductive part of work life. How did something central to leadership and collaboration become synonymous with inefficiency and frustration?

The truth is that meetings are not inherently flawed. When approached with intention and skill, they can be transformative. Effective meetings provide clarity, foster alignment, and build momentum toward achieving organizational goals. They serve as a space where diverse perspectives converge, challenges are tackled, and creativity flourishes. In many ways, mastering meetings is about mastering leadership itself.

This book is designed to help leaders do just that through practical strategies, reflective prompts, and storytelling. Mastering Meetings: A Journal for Effective Leadership will guide you in turning meetings into powerful tools for connection and progress. Whether you are a seasoned executive, a team lead, or a rising leader, this book will equip you with the skills and mindset needed to lead with purpose and inspire action.

The Journey Ahead

In the following chapters, you will explore the critical elements of effective meetings, from setting clear objectives and fostering inclusivity to managing conflicts and tracking progress. You'll meet Maya, a leader navigating team collaboration challenges, and follow her story as she learns to transform her meetings and leadership style. Her journey is designed to reflect the real-world complexities leaders face, offering relatable and actionable lessons.

Each chapter will present insights, techniques, and opportunities to reflect on your practices. The accompanying journal prompts will encourage you to identify strengths, confront challenges, and continuously improve your meeting approach. By the end of this book, you will have a deeper understanding of effective meeting practices and a personalized blueprint for leading with confidence and clarity.

Why This Matters Now

In an era where organizations are increasingly global, diverse, and fast-paced, the ability to conduct meaningful and impactful meetings has never been more critical. Leaders are tasked with bringing together individuals from different backgrounds, navigating virtual and in-person dynamics, and achieving alignment amidst constant change. Meetings are the thread that weaves these elements together, and mastering them is no longer optional—it's essential.

This book is your companion on that journey. Whether grappling with unproductive meetings, aiming to improve collaboration, or striving to lead with greater intention, Mastering Meetings offers the tools and insights you need to elevate your leadership and unlock your team's potential.

So, let's begin. Together, we'll reimagine what meetings can be and how they can serve as a catalyst for your growth as a leader—and for your organization's success.

Understanding the Role of Meetings in Leadership

The Monday Morning Wake-Up Call

As the meeting began, Maya's confidence quickly evaporated. The first 20 minutes were a mess of cross-talk and side conversations. Rahul, the tech lead, was bottomless in a monologue about server migration, while Ella, the junior marketer, raised her hand hesitantly, hoping someone would notice. Daniel, the operations head, leaned back in his chair, smirking as if he had a running tally of every wasted minute.

By the time the hour was up, nothing had been decided, and everyone left the room more confused than when they entered. Maya slumped back in her chair, staring at the scattered notes on her laptop. How can I lead when I can't even run a meeting?

That's when she heard a voice from the door. "Rough start, huh?" It was Alex Walker, the company's leadership coach. Known for turning chaos into clarity, Alex had a reputation for showing up at just the right moment. Calm and confident, Alex walked in, grabbed a marker, and began sketching on the whiteboard.

"Let me tell you something, Maya," Alex began. "Meetings aren't just a place to dump information or argue over problems. They're where leadership happens."

Maya blinked, unsure of what Alex meant. "Leadership? I thought meetings were about collaboration and communication."

"Exactly," Alex replied. "Leadership through collaboration, communication, and decision-making. Meetings are your chance to align your team, resolve conflicts, and inspire action."

Alex outlined three principles on the board: Alignment, Conflict Resolution, and Inspiration.

"These three elements," Alex explained, "separate a productive meeting from a waste of time. Without alignment, your team is just a group working on their priorities. Conflict resolution ensures differences don't derail progress, and inspiration keeps the team motivated and focused."

Maya nodded, taking notes. It was the first time she saw meetings as more than tasks on her to-do list—they were opportunities to lead.

"First, meetings align your team with the organizational goals. Without that alignment, you're just twelve individuals chasing their priorities. Second, they're where you deal with conflicts—not just disagreements, but misunderstandings or competing priorities. And finally, meetings are where you set the tone for the team's energy and purpose. You've got to inspire them to believe in the vision."

Maya frowned. "But how do I get there? Today was a disaster."

"That's because you're focusing on the wrong things," Alex said. "You're trying to control the chaos instead of creating structure. Let's start with something simple: define the purpose of your meeting. What's the one thing you wanted to accomplish today?"

Maya paused, realizing she hadn't been clear about her own goals for the meeting.

Alex continued, "Meetings serve several roles in leadership, and understanding these roles is essential for fostering a productive environment. Here's what you need to know:

Structured Dialogue: Effective meetings allow all voices to be heard. When diverse perspectives are encouraged, discussions become richer, fostering creative problem-solving and innovation.

Conflict Resolution: Meetings allow you to address tensions directly. Differences in opinion, misunderstandings, and competing priorities can disrupt a team. However, when handled skillfully, these conflicts become opportunities for growth and collaboration.

Goal Setting and Accountability: Meetings are where you set objectives and assign responsibilities. Without the discussion become rhetoric, and nothing gets accomplished."

Maya nodded as Alex handed her a notebook. It was time to rethink her approach to leadership, starting with her meetings.

Here's what I want you to do before the next meeting," Alex continued. "Write down three things:

- Your Meeting Objective: What's the purpose of the meeting?
- Your Team's Input: Who needs to contribute, and how will they do it?
- Your End Goal: What do you want to walk away with?"

Maya scribbled the steps down, her thoughts shifting from frustration to determination.

"Remember," Alex said, "every meeting is a mirror of your leadership. If it's messy, unclear, or unfocused, it reflects how you're leading your team. But when you bring clarity, structure, and purpose, you inspire trust and productivity."

At the end of the chapter, consider these questions to apply what you've learned:

- What habits or practices can I adopt to ensure purposeful and inspiring meetings?
- How do my current meetings reflect my leadership style, and what adjustments can I make?
- What specific outcomes do I want my meetings to achieve?
- What role do meetings play in your leadership style?
- How can you make your next meeting purposeful,

inclusive, and inspiring?

- What steps can I take to ensure all participants feel included and prepared?
- How do I prepare my team to contribute effectively to the meeting's goals?
- Are my meeting objectives clear and aligned with team priorities?
- What's one habit you can start today to improve your meeting outcomes?

By mastering the dynamics of meetings, you'll guide your team to better outcomes and grow as a leader who fosters collaboration, accountability, and innovation.

Preparing for Success

The Turning Point

Behind every successful meeting is careful preparation. The best leaders understand that impactful meetings don't happen by chance—they result from thoughtful planning, intentional goal-setting, and a clear focus on outcome Without preparation, meetings risk becoming unfocused, leaving participants disengaged and valuable time wasted.

Preparation is not just about logistics; it's about aligning purpose with action. It's about ensuring every meeting has a defined objective, the right participants, and the tools to foster meaningful discussions. When leaders prepare effectively, they create an environment where ideas flow, decisions are made, and teams leave feeling empowered and aligned.

In this chapter, we'll explore the foundational steps to set the stage for a productive meeting. From crafting clear objectives and agendas to choosing the right participants and leveraging tools for collaboration, preparation is where the seeds of success are sown.

Through Maya's journey, you'll see the transformative power of preparation in action. You'll learn how a few deliberate steps can shift meetings from chaotic and frustrating to purposeful and engaging. You'll also discover practical strategies and reflective prompts to help you refine your preparation practices, ensuring your meetings are always focused, inclusive, and impactful.

Preparing for success isn't just a task; it's a mindset. Let's dive in and explore how you can lay the groundwork for meetings that inspire collaboration, creativity, and results.

The following day, Alex stopped by her office, notebook in hand. "Let me tell you a story," Alex began, sitting across from Maya.

"There was a team tasked with designing a new product. Their meetings were always chaotic. People spoke over each other, decisions were never made, and morale was low. Sound familiar?"

Maya smiled ruefully. "Too familiar."

"One day, the team's leader decided to try something new. Before their next meeting, she sent out a clear agenda with three specific objectives. She clarified what they were coming to discuss and what decisions needed to be made. The result was transformative. The meeting stayed on track for the first time, and the team left with a concrete plan."

Maya leaned forward. "So, the key is objectives?"

"Absolutely," Alex said. "Without them, meetings meander, frustrations rise, and nothing gets accomplished. Objectives give a meeting its purpose. They're the North Star that keeps everyone focused.

Understanding the Importance of Clear Objectives
Alex handed Maya a fresh notepad. "Here's what I want you to think about as you plan your next meeting."

Define the Purpose

"Before calling a meeting, ask yourself: What's the primary purpose? Are you making a decision, brainstorming ideas, or sharing critical updates? If you can't define the purpose, the meeting probably isn't necessary."

Encourage Preparation

"When objectives are clear, people come prepared. Participants can gather the right data, insights, or questions if they know the goals. This leads to richer discussions and more engaged attendees."

Foster Accountability

"Objectives aren't just about setting a direction; they're about ownership. When team members understand what's expected of them, they feel more accountable for their contributions during and after the meeting."

Promote Inclusion

"By inviting input from diverse perspectives while setting objectives, you ensure no voice goes unheard. This enriches discussions and builds buy-in and commitment to the outcomes."

Maya furrowed her brow. "Okay, I get the importance of objectives. But how do I make sure they drive the meeting?"

Alex flipped open his notebook. "An effective agenda is your secret weapon. Here's how you do it:"

Align Agenda Items with Objectives

"List your meeting objectives first. Then, structure the agenda to prioritize the topics that align with those goals. Don't let unrelated items steal the spotlight."

Allocate Time Wisely

"Give each topic a realistic time slot. Respect everyone's schedule while allowing enough time for meaningful discussions. Don't be afraid to cut off tangents—keep the meeting focused."

Share the Agenda in Advance

"Send the agenda along with the objectives before the meeting. When people know what's coming, they're better prepared to contribute."

Inviting the Right Participants

"Now," Alex continued, "let's talk about who should be at the table."

Diversity Drives Innovation "Invite people with diverse perspectives. A mix of backgrounds, experiences, and expertise fosters creativity and better problem-solving."

"Don't invite everyone just because they're available. Focus on participants with the knowledge or authority to contribute meaningfully to the objectives."

"Identify team members who can mediate or bring calm to heated discussions. A good mix of personalities can prevent conflict from derailing progress."

"After each meeting, think about who contributed most effectively and who might not need to be there next time. Adjust your invitations accordingly."

Maya flipped open her notebook. With Alex's guidance, she wrote down three objectives for her next meeting:

- Finalize the timeline for the product launch.
- Identify roadblocks in the design phase.
- Assign ownership for action items related to marketing.

"That's it," Alex said. "Simple, clear, and actionable. Share these objectives and your agenda with the team before the meeting. Then, watch what happens."

At the end of the chapter, Alex left Maya with these words: "Objectives are the foundation of a productive meeting. Without them, you're wandering in the dark. With them, you can lead your team with purpose and clarity."

- How do I handle conflicts constructively during discussions?
- What strategies can I use to balance participation and manage dominating voices?
- How can I create an environment where everyone feels comfortable sharing ideas?

Reflect On:

- What objectives do I need to clarify for my next meeting?
- How can I ensure these objectives align with my team's goals and priorities?
- Am I inviting the right people to contribute meaningfully to the discussion?

Leaders can transform their meetings into powerful tools for alignment, accountability, and innovation by mastering the art of setting objectives and creating purposeful agendas.

Facilitating Productive Discussions

Voices in the Room

The conference room buzzed with chatter as Maya walked in, notepad in hand. Today's meeting has a clear agenda and objectives—thanks to Alex's guidance—but Maya still felt a pang of doubt. Would she be able to keep the discussion on track? Would everyone feel heard?

Her thoughts were interrupted as Alex leaned against the wall casually. "Ready to lead this discussion?" Alex asked with a knowing smile.

"I think so," Maya said hesitantly. "I've set the objectives and shared the agenda. But what happens when the conversation goes off the rails? Or worse, when some people dominate, and others stay silent?"

Alex nodded. "Good questions. Let me tell you about a leader I worked with who faced the same challenge."

"There was a manager named Grace who led a team of dynamic, ambitious professionals. Every meeting turned into a battleground of strong opinions, while quieter voices never got a chance to speak. As a result, the team missed out on some brilliant ideas—and morale started to drop.

"To address this, Grace did three things:

- *Set Ground Rules for Discussions*
  At the start of every meeting, she reminded the team of their shared values: respect, open-mindedness, and constructive dialogue. These rules created a safe space for everyone to contribute.

- *Encouraged Balanced Participation*
  Grace used round-robin sharing and breakout groups to ensure everyone's voice was heard. She introduced anonymous question submissions, especially for shy team members, to boost confidence.

- *Handled Conflict Constructively*
  Grace didn't shy away from disagreements. Instead, she reframed conflicts as opportunities to explore different perspectives. She guided the team to shared goals, keeping discussions focused and collaborative."

Alex leaned forward. "By implementing these practices, Grace transformed her meetings and built a stronger, more inclusive team."

"Here's the thing," Alex said. "Facilitating productive discussions isn't just about keeping order—it's about creating a space where ideas can flourish. And that starts with you."

Alex outlined key steps Maya could take:

Set the Tone

"Begin every meeting by stating its purpose and ground rules. Respect and openness should be non-negotiable."

Guide the Conversation

"Use your agenda as a guide, but stay flexible. Keep the discussion focused, and gently steer it back when it veers off track."

Encourage Diverse Perspectives

"Actively invite input from quieter team members. Sometimes, the best ideas come from the voices that aren't immediately heard."

Manage Dominating Voices

"If someone starts monopolizing the conversation, thank them for their input and invite others to share their thoughts."

Handle Conflict with Grace

"When tensions rise, remind the team of your shared objectives. Reframe disagreements as opportunities for growth, and focus on finding solutions."

Maya furiously jotted down notes as Alex continued.

"To keep everyone engaged, mix things up. Here are some techniques to try:

- **Breakout Sessions**: Divide the team into smaller groups to tackle specific topics, then reconvene to share insights.

- **Live Polls**: Use digital tools to collect real-time feedback, especially for sensitive topics.
- **Interactive Brainstorming**: Encourage collaboration with activities like mind mapping or rapid-fire idea generation."

Alex paused. "But remember, it's not just about keeping people busy. Engagement happens when people feel valued. That means fostering inclusion. Diversity and inclusion aren't just buzzwords—they're the secret ingredients for innovation," Alex said. "To create an inclusive meeting culture:

Proactively seek input from underrepresented voices.

Rotate facilitators to give everyone a chance to lead. Use anonymous feedback tools to ensure everyone feels

safe contributing."

Maya nodded. "That makes sense. But what about after the meeting?"

"Great question," Alex said. "Reflection is how you get better. After every meeting, ask yourself:

What worked well?

What could be improved?

Did everyone feel heard?

"Then, follow up. Summarize key decisions and action items, and hold the team accountable. When people see their input driving results, they'll stay engaged."

- What techniques can I apply to turn disagreements into opportunities for growth?

- How can I ensure my response to conflict fosters collaboration and understanding?
- What potential sources of conflict can I identify and address proactively?

As Maya prepared for the discussion, she felt a newfound confidence. She began the meeting by welcoming everyone and outlining the ground rules: respect, collaboration, and focus. She used the agenda to keep the team on track and invited quieter members to share their thoughts.

By the end, the team had achieved their objectives and left the room energized and connected. Maya realized that facilitating productive discussions wasn't about controlling the conversation but guiding it with intention and care.

At the end of the chapter, Alex left Maya with these reminders:

- How can I create a safe space for diverse perspectives in my meetings?
- What techniques can I use to ensure balanced participation?
- How can I reflect on and improve my facilitation skills after each meeting?

Resolving Conflict in Meetings

Finding Common Ground

Maya sat at the head of the table, watching as the tension in the room thickened. Rahul and Daniel were locked in a heated exchange, their voices rising with each rebuttal. Sitting in the corner, Ella looked down at her notebook, clearly uncomfortable. The meeting had started with good intentions, but now it felt like a battleground.

Alex stepped into the room just as Maya was about to intervene. With a calm but firm tone, Alex said, "Alright, let's pause here. Maya, come with me for a moment."

In the hallway, Alex turned to Maya. "What you just witnessed isn't unusual. Conflict is inevitable in meetings, but it doesn't have to derail progress. Let's unpack what might be causing it."

Alex outlined the familiar sources of conflict:

Communication Barriers - "Sometimes, it's not what people say, but how they say it. Misunderstandings in tone, body language, or phrasing can lead to unnecessary friction. Add cultural differences, and it's easy for people to feel misunderstood or dismissed."

Differing Objectives - "Everyone comes to a meeting with their priorities. When those priorities clash, tension builds. That's why it's essential to set clear, collective goals upfront."

Personality Clashes - "People approach discussions differently some are analytical, others are emotional. Without understanding these differences, teams can struggle to work together effectively."

External Stressors - "Deadlines, workload, or personal challenges can make people more reactive. Acknowledging these pressures can help diffuse unnecessary conflict."

Maya nodded, taking notes. "So, how do I handle it when conflict happens?"

Alex smiled. "Conflict isn't always bad. If handled well, it can lead to growth and stronger outcomes. Here's what you can do."

Active Listening

"When tensions rise, your first job is to listen—listen. Let each person explain their perspective without interruption. Then, paraphrase what they've said to show you understand. This simple act of validation can lower defenses and open the door to productive dialogue."

Set Ground Rules

"At the start of every meeting, establish expectations for respectful communication. Remind the team to focus on issues, not personalities. And if someone crosses a line, don't hesitate to reinforce those rules."

Break into Smaller Groups

"If the discussion gets too heated, split the team into smaller groups. Smaller settings are less intimidating and encourage more open, constructive conversations. You can reconvene once emotions have settled."

Use Neutral Mediation

"When the conflict feels too big to handle at the moment, bring in a neutral third party—like me," Alex said with a grin. "Mediators can help guide the conversation to shared goals and mutual understanding."

Reframe the Conflict

"Instead of seeing disagreements as obstacles, frame them as learning opportunities. Highlight the shared goals that brought everyone to the table and use those to steer the discussion forward."

Maya took a deep breath and reentered the room with Alex. She addressed the group, "Alright, let's pause momentarily. I want to make sure everyone feels heard. Rahul, can you share your perspective first? Then we'll hear from Daniel."

As each spoke, Maya listened attentively, paraphrasing key points to ensure clarity. "It sounds like Rahul is concerned about the timeline, while Daniel wants to ensure the quality of the deliverables. Both are valid points, and we're all committed to the project's success. Let's find a way to address both concerns."

- How do I create a meeting culture where everyone feels valued and respected?
- What specific actions can I take to address power dynamics and ensure balanced participation?
- How can I actively encourage diverse perspectives in my meetings?

Alex asked, "Why don't we break into smaller groups to brainstorm solutions? Maya and I will float between groups to support."

The team divided, and the tension in the room visibly eased. By the time they reconvened, they had actionable solutions and a renewed sense of collaboration.

After the meeting, Alex shared a few final thoughts with Maya:

Conflict isn't inherently wrong. It's an opportunity to surface important issues and strengthen the team. De-escalation starts with you. Your tone, approach, and ability to listen set the example.

Always bring it back to shared goals. Remind the team of what unites them, not what divides them.

Reflect On:

- What strategies can I use to identify and address sources of conflict in my meetings?
- How can I ensure all perspectives are valued during tense discussions?
- What ground rules can I establish to foster a respectful and productive meeting culture?

Diversity and Inclusion in Meetings

The Power of Different Perspectives

Maya looked around the table. The team was diverse—different ages, backgrounds, and perspectives—but something felt off. A few voices dominated every meeting, while others barely spoke. She wanted to unlock the full potential of her team, but she wasn't sure how to bring everyone into the conversation.

Frustrated, she called Alex.

"Struggling to balance the room?" Alex asked after Maya explained the situation.

"Exactly," Maya said. "How do I ensure everyone feels heard without forcing them to talk?"

Alex smiled. "Let me tell you about Jordan, a leader who faced a similar challenge."

Jordan managed a diverse team responsible for launching a new product. Despite their differences in culture, experience, and backgrounds, only a few team members consistently contributed. Others stayed quiet, unsure if their ideas were valued.

Jordan took three key steps to shift the team dynamic:

- *Set the Stage for Inclusivity*
  Jordan created ground rules that encouraged participation, emphasizing that every idea was valuable. This established a safe environment for sharing.

- *Engaged Everyone Actively*
  Techniques like round-robin sharing and anonymous idea submissions helped even reserved team members contribute.

- *Leveled the Playing Field*
  By rotating facilitators and addressing power dynamics, Jordan ensured everyone had a chance to lead and participate equally.

The results were transformative. The team became more cohesive and innovative as everyone felt their input mattered.

"Here's the thing, Maya," Alex said. "Diversity isn't just about who's in the room—it's about engaging them. By embracing different perspectives, you unlock creativity, innovation, and better decision-making."

Alex broke it down further:

- *Diverse Teams Bring Unique Insights*: Different backgrounds lead to richer discussions and solutions.

- *Psychological Safety is Essential*: People need to feel

safe sharing ideas, even if they challenge the norm.

- *Conflict Can Drive Growth*: Differences can create friction, but when managed, that friction sparks deeper understanding and innovation.

"Creating an inclusive culture takes effort, but it's worth it," Alex added.

Here's how to start:

- **Set Clear Expectations**: Define ground rules for respect and open communication.
- **Address Dynamics**: Acknowledge how power or cultural differences impact participation and guide discussions to ensure balance.
- **Invest in Training**: Provide emotional intelligence and cultural competence training to empower the team.
- **Solicit Feedback**: Regularly ask for input on meeting inclusivity and adapt based on feedback.

"What about clashing perspectives?" Maya asked.

Alex grinned. "That's where the magic happens—if you manage it well. Conflict isn't the enemy; it's an opportunity for growth."

- **Reframe Conflict**: When opinions differ, explore the reasons behind them. Replace defensiveness with curiosity.
- **Encourage Respectful Debate**: Create ground rules for disagreements, focusing on understanding rather than winning.
- **Document and Act**: Assign follow-up tasks to ensure

ideas are implemented.

At her next meeting, Maya applied Alex's advice. She set the tone: "Today, let's brainstorm solutions. Everyone, share at least one idea—big or small."

Using a round-robin format, Maya ensured each person had equal time to speak. For those hesitant to share, she introduced a digital tool for anonymous submissions.

When disagreements arose, she guided the team back to their shared goals. "We're all here to solve the same problem," she reminded them. "Let's explore these differences together."

By the end of the meeting, the team had generated a variety of innovative ideas, and everyone left feeling heard and valued.

Alex reminded Maya that diversity and inclusion are the foundation of effective leadership—not just buzzwords.

Consider these questions:

- How can I create a meeting culture where all voices are heard?
- What techniques can I use to address power dynamics and encourage balanced participation?
- How can I turn conflict into a catalyst for innovation?

By embracing diversity and fostering engagement, leaders can transform meetings into spaces of creativity, collaboration, and growth.

Personal Reflection for Meeting Leaders

Lessons in Leadership

Maya sat in her office, staring at her notebook. The meeting earlier in the day had gone smoothly, but something about it gnawed at her. Had she made the right call during the tense discussion between Rahul and Ella? Had she created enough space for quieter team members to contribute?

She sighed and picked up her phone. Alex's voice on the other end was calm and reassuring. "It sounds like you're asking the right questions," Alex said. "Let me tell you a story about a leader who mastered meetings by learning to reflect."

"There was a manager named Sofia who was known for her ambitious projects but often struggled to bring her team together. After one particularly chaotic meeting, she decided to make a change.

"Sofia began by asking her team for feedback. She wondered what worked, what didn't, and how she could improve. At first, the responses were generic—people hesitated to critique their boss. But as Sofia showed she was serious about making changes over time, her team began to open up.

"She also started keeping a personal reflection journal. After every meeting, she wrote down three things:

What went well?

What could have been better?

What would she do differently next time?

"This practice gave her insights into her leadership style, helped her spot patterns, and showed her how to adapt her approach based on the needs of her team."

Alex paused. "Maya, reflection is one of the most powerful tools for a leader. To grow, you need to understand how your leadership style affects your team."

Alex explained how to begin:

Seek Feedback

"Ask your team what they think of your leadership during meetings. Use anonymous surveys or informal check-ins to get honest insights."

Reflect on Your Reactions

"Consider how you handle different scenarios—conflict, disagreements, or silence. Are you directing the conversation or facilitating dialogue? Your instincts will show you where you need to grow."

Learn from Leadership Models

"Explore different leadership styles, like transformational or servant leadership, and compare them to your approach. This can highlight strengths and reveal areas for improvement."

"Choose one or two areas to focus on, like improving inclusivity or managing conflicts. Track your progress over time."

Maya nodded, scribbling notes. "But what about the meetings themselves? How do I know if they're effective?"

Alex smiled. "Every meeting is a learning opportunity. Here's how to reflect on them:

"Did everyone have a chance to speak? Were diverse perspectives included? If certain voices dominate, think about how to balance the conversation next time."

"When disagreements arose, how were they handled? Did the team work through the issue constructively, or were tensions left unresolved?"

"Were the meeting's objectives clear? Did the team leave with actionable steps? Use the SMART framework to evaluate whether goals were specific, measurable, achievable, relevant, and time-bound. Think about your performance. Did you guide the discussion effectively? Did you foster collaboration and inclusivity?"

Alex leaned back. "The key to becoming a great leader, Maya, is embracing a growth mindset. This means seeing every challenge, every mistake, and every meeting as an opportunity to learn. Create a culture where team members feel safe giving and receiving feedback. Model this behavior by being open about your areas for growth. Recognize that diverse

perspectives make meetings richer. Actively seek out different viewpoints and value them, even when they challenge your assumptions."

"Approach conflicts and failures with curiosity.

Ask, 'What can I learn from this?' rather than, 'Why did this happen?' Push yourself and your team to grow. Set realistic but ambitious objectives that inspire progress and innovation."

Maya thanked Alex and hung up. She opened her notebook and began jotting down her thoughts about the day's meeting:

- What went well? Ella had shared a new idea, and the team embraced it.

- What could have been better? Rahul had dominated the discussion at one point, and Maya hadn't stepped in soon enough.

- What will I do differently? Next time, Maya would use a round-robin format to ensure everyone had a chance to speak.

As she closed her notebook, Maya felt a sense of clarity. Reflection wasn't just about fixing mistakes, growing as a leader, and building a stronger, more cohesive team.

Alex's final advice to Maya was simple but powerful:

- How does my leadership style impact my team during meetings?

- What patterns can I identify from past meetings that I need to address?

- How can I model a growth mindset to inspire my team?

By committing to personal reflection and continuous learning, leaders can transform their meetings—and themselves.

Goal Setting and Accountability in Meetings

From Goals to Growth

Maya stood at the front of the room, glancing at the agenda she'd prepared. Today's meeting was pivotal—Maya's team needed to finalize the product launch timeline and resolve lingering roadblocks. As the team gathered, Maya took a deep breath, determined to keep the discussion productive.

"Alright, team," she began. "Let's revisit our focus. Today, we'll finalize the launch timeline and address any outstanding challenges. This isn't just about completing the agenda but driving progress toward our organizational objectives."

By consistently tying each topic back to the team's shared goals, Maya ensured the discussion stayed on track. By the meeting's end, everyone left with clear next steps and a renewed sense of purpose.

Later, Alex stopped by her office.

"How did it feel leading today's meeting?" Alex asked.

"Better," Maya admitted. "But I feel like I'm still missing something when it comes to aligning goals and holding the team accountable."

Alex nodded. "Let's dig into that."

"Every meeting needs a clear purpose," Alex explained. "But it's not enough to have a purpose—you need to align it with the organization's broader goals."

Alex outlined the process:

1. **Understand Organizational Priorities**
   - Identify your company's key performance indicators, strategic goals, and long-term vision.
   - For example, if innovation is a priority, structure meetings to foster creative problem-solving and brainstorming.

2. **Translate Objectives into Actionable Goals**
   - Break down big-picture objectives into specific, measurable outcomes.
   - Instead of vague goals like "improve marketing," aim for concrete actions such as "outline three ideas for the next campaign."

3. **Foster Inclusivity for Broader Perspectives**
   - Diverse teams offer richer discussions. Create opportunities for everyone to contribute and ensure their ideas align with larger goals.

4. **Address Conflicts Constructively**
   - Conflict is inevitable but can refocus the team if handled well. Always steer discussions back to the meeting's purpose and organizational objectives.

"How do I ensure everyone follows through on their commitments?" Maya asked.

"Accountability is essential," Alex replied. "Here's how to build it into your meetings."

1. Define Clear Outcomes
   o At the end of each meeting, clearly articulate success criteria. Assign specific action items, set deadlines, and confirm responsibilities.
2. Use Regular Check-Ins
   o Follow up on action items in subsequent meetings to track progress and keep momentum.
3. Create a Culture of Trust
   o Encourage open communication. When team members feel supported, they're more likely to own their tasks and raise challenges early.
4. Recognize Achievements
   o Celebrate small wins to reinforce accountability and keep the team motivated.

"But how do I know if a meeting was successful?" Maya asked.

"Great question," Alex said. "Evaluating outcomes is as important as setting goals. Consider these factors:"

1. **Measure Against Objectives**
   - Did the meeting achieve its intended goals? Were these goals tied to organizational priorities?
2. **Gather Feedback**
   - Use surveys or informal conversations to understand team perceptions of clarity and engagement,
3. **Assess Decision-Making**
   - Were decisions actionable? Did participants leave knowing their next steps?
4. **Promote Inclusivity**

- Ensure everyone had a chance to contribute, and that diverse perspectives were considered in decisions.

Maya no longer saw meetings as routine discussions but as strategic tools for driving progress. For her next meeting, she took proactive steps:

- Clearly articulated the meeting's purpose and its connection to company goals.
- Assigned specific action items with deadlines.
- Followed up with team members to ensure accountability.

As a result, Maya's team felt more aligned and energized. They understood how their work contributed directly to the organization's success.

Alex left Maya with three questions to consider:

- How can I ensure my meeting goals align with my organization's objectives?
- What accountability mechanisms can I implement to drive follow-through?
- How can I evaluate my meetings to improve future outcomes?

By setting clear goals, fostering accountability, and continuously refining their approach, leaders can transform meetings into powerful tools for organizational growth.

Continuous Improvement

The Feedback Loop

Maya sat in her office, staring at her computer screen. The last meeting had been productive, but she couldn't shake the feeling that something was missing. Not everyone left the room feeling heard or engaged, and she wanted to do better.

Picking up the phone, she called Alex.

"Let me guess," Alex said with a chuckle. "You're wondering how to make good meetings even better."

"Exactly," Maya admitted. "How do I know what's working and what isn't?"

"That's where feedback comes in," Alex said. "Let me share a story about a leader who mastered the art of gathering and acting on feedback."

"There was a manager named Rachel who prided herself on running efficient meetings. But one day, she overheard her team complaining that their voices weren't being valued.

"That was her wake-up call. Rachel began asking for feedback after every meeting. At first, it was simple—anonymous surveys with questions like, 'Did this meeting achieve its objectives?' and, 'What could have been better?'

"Patterns started to emerge. Some team members felt rushed, others overshadowed by louder voices, and many wanted clearer follow-ups on action items.

"Rachel acted on the feedback. She made discussions more balanced, clarified goals, and ensured consistent follow-ups. Over time, her team became more engaged, and meetings became opportunities to collaborate rather than obligations."

"Feedback is your secret weapon," Alex said. "Here's how to use it effectively:"

1. **Start with Post-Meeting Surveys**
   - Include quantitative questions (e.g., rate the meeting's effectiveness) and qualitative ones (e.g., suggestions for improvement).

2. **Create a Safe Environment**
   - Offer anonymous options to encourage honest feedback, especially for quieter team members.

3. **Proactively Seek Input**
   - Directly ask, "What did you think?" to invite insights from those who might not volunteer feedback.

4. **Look for Patterns**
   - o Identify recurring themes in the feedback to pinpoint what's working and what isn't.

5. **Act on Feedback**
   - o Share what you've learned with the team and outline the changes you'll implement. This builds trust and shows their input is valued.

Best Practices for Effective Meetings

Maya leaned forward, taking notes. "But how do I ensure I consistently apply what I've learned?"

Alex smiled. "That's where best practices come in."

1. **Plan with Precision**
   - o Every meeting should have a clear agenda and defined objectives. Share these in advance so participants can prepare.

2. **Invite the Right People**
   - o Focus on those with a stake in the discussion or unique perspectives to share. Prioritize diversity to enrich conversations.

3. **Facilitate Effectively**
   - o Keep discussions focused, manage conflicts constructively, and encourage everyone to participate. Use active listening and open-ended questions to foster collaboration.

4. **Follow Up**
   - o Assign clear action items with deadlines. Revisit these in subsequent meetings to ensure progress.

5. **Reflect and Refine**

- o After every meeting, ask yourself: Did we meet our objectives? Did everyone contribute? How can I improve next time?

Adapting to Change

"But what happens when things change—new technology, new team members, new goals?" Maya asked.

"That's where adaptability comes in," Alex replied.

1. **Leverage Technology**
   - o Use tools like virtual platforms, live polls, or shared documents to make meetings more inclusive and efficient.

2. **Understand Your Team**
   - o Adapt to the diverse cultural backgrounds and communication styles within your team to ensure everyone feels included.

3. **Revisit Goals Regularly**
   - o Adjust meeting agendas to align with evolving organizational priorities.

4. **Stay Flexible**
   - o Experiment with new formats or techniques to keep meetings relevant and effective.

At her next meeting, Maya tried something new. She handed out a brief survey at the end with three simple questions:

- What did you find most valuable about this meeting?
- What could be improved?
- What's one thing you'd like to see in future meetings?

The responses were eye-opening. Some team members wanted more time to prepare for discussions, while others suggested rotating facilitation roles to give everyone a chance to lead. Maya implemented these changes and noticed an immediate shift. Meetings became more dynamic, and the team felt more invested.

Reflection Points

Alex left Maya with three key questions to consider:

- How can I create a feedback process that encourages honest input?
- What best practices can I implement to make my meetings more effective?
- How can I adapt my meeting strategies to address the evolving needs of my team?

By committing to continuous improvement, leaders can transform meetings into impactful tools that align with the needs of their teams and organizations.

.

Technology to Enhance Engagement

The Digital Connection

Maya noticed her team's energy waning during the virtual meeting. Some participants seemed engaged, while others appeared distracted. Unsure how to reinvigorate the discussion, she picked up the phone and called Alex.

"How do I make virtual meetings as dynamic as in-person ones?" she asked.

Alex smiled. "The answer lies in the tools you use. Technology can transform your meetings into truly interactive experiences. Technology isn't just about enabling remote participation," Alex explained. "It's about fostering deeper engagement and inclusivity. Platforms like Zoom and Microsoft Teams offers features beyond basic video calls. Use:

- **Breakout Rooms** for smaller group discussions.
- **Polls** to gauge opinions in real-time.
- **Chat Functions** to encourage quieter participants to share their thoughts."

"These features bridge the gap between remote and in-person attendees, fostering a sense of cohesion."

Collaborative Platforms

"Visual tools like Miro and Trello allow teams to brainstorm and organize ideas collaboratively. Watching concepts evolve on a shared board makes discussions more engaging and easier to follow."

"Shared documents in Google Workspace or Microsoft 365 let participants contribute edits and comments in real-time, ensuring everyone has a voice."

Engagement Analytics

"Analytics features on some platforms can reveal participation trends. If certain team members aren't contributing, follow up directly or adjust your facilitation to draw them in. Technology can also make meetings more inclusive," Alex continued. Features like live transcription, closed captioning or language translation tools ensure full participation, regardless of hearing abilities or language proficiency."

Anonymous Feedback

"Tools that allow anonymous questions or comments encourage input from those who might hesitate to speak up."

Rotating Roles

"Have team members take turns leading brainstorming sessions or updating shared boards. This builds inclusivity and ensures everyone feels involved."

"Technology doesn't stop when the meeting ends," Alex said. "The right tools help ensure follow-through."

Project Management Platforms

"Tools like Jira or Monday.com track tasks and deadlines set during meetings, so everyone knows what they're responsible for and when it's due."

Automated Follow-Ups

"Platforms can send summaries, action items, and reminders automatically, helping to keep everyone aligned."

Progress Tracking

"Dashboards monitor task progress, providing visual accountability to keep teams motivated and on track."

At her next virtual meeting, Maya incorporated Alex's advice:

- **Started with a Poll** to prioritize discussion topics.

- **Map** ideas in real-time during brainstorming.

- **Assigned Tasks in Jira** and set follow-up reminders.

The results were immediate. The meeting felt more dynamic, and the team left energized and clear on their next steps.

Alex left Maya with these questions to consider:

- How can I use technology to make my meetings more interactive and inclusive?

- What tools can I implement to support goal-setting and accountability?

- How can I leverage analytics to understand better and improve team engagement?

By embracing technology's possibilities, leaders can transform their meetings into spaces of collaboration, innovation, and growth.

Setting Personal Meeting Goals

The Compass for Success

Maya sat at her desk, pen in hand, staring at a blank notepad. She had been running meetings for months, but something felt off. Action items were assigned, yet the sense of alignment and purpose she longed for seemed elusive. Frustrated, she picked up the phone and called Alex.

"What's your intention for these meetings?" Alex asked.

"To get things done," Maya replied, hesitating.

Alex chuckled. "Getting things done is a result, not an intention. Let's start by setting personal meeting goals. Think of them as your compass—they guide the team toward meaningful outcomes."

"Personal meeting goals help leaders focus on the 'why' behind the meeting," Alex explained.

1. **Align Goals with Context**

- o "Each meeting serves a unique purpose—brainstorming, conflict resolution, or project updates. Tailor your goals to the context. For example, if resolving a conflict, focus on fostering open communication and understanding diverse perspectives."

2. **Prioritize Relevance and Engagement**
   - o "Define clear, actionable objectives to keep discussions focused and participants engaged."

3. **Embed Inclusivity**
   - o "Incorporate diversity into your goals. Rotate facilitators, set equal speaking time guidelines, or actively invite input from quieter team members."

Maya jotted notes as Alex continued.

1. **Evaluate Past Experiences**
   - o "Ask yourself: What worked well in previous meetings? What didn't? Were objectives clear? Did participants leave with purpose?"

2. **Adjust Your Leadership Style**
   - o "Reflect on your approach. Did you dominate the conversation or create space for collaboration? Self-awareness helps refine your strategy."

3. **Set Realistic, Actionable Goals**
   - o "Avoid vague objectives like 'improve engagement.' Instead, target specific outcomes like 'gather three actionable ideas for the next marketing campaign.'"

Fostering Accountability

"But how do I ensure the goals stick?" Maya asked.

"Accountability is key," Alex replied.

1. **Communicate Objectives Clearly**
   - o "Start meetings by outlining their purpose and goals. Transparency aligns efforts and sets expectations."
2. **Encourage Collective Responsibility**
   - o "Make goal achievement a team effort. Encourage participants to hold each other accountable."
3. **Track Progress**
   - o "Revisit goals at the meeting's end. Summarize achievements and assign follow-ups to reinforce accountability."

"Goals are just the beginning," Alex said. "You need a roadmap to turn them into reality."

1. **Define Specific Objectives**
   - o "Identify what the meeting should accomplish and how it supports broader organizational goals."
2. **Involve the Right Participants**
   - o "Invite individuals with relevant expertise and diverse perspectives. This fosters richer collaboration."
3. **Assign Responsibilities**
   - o "Break goals into tasks, assign them to team members, and set deadlines to ensure follow-through."
4. **Implement Follow-Ups**

- o "Schedule check-ins to track progress, address challenges, and maintain momentum."

"Don't forget to measure success," Alex added. "And celebrate it!"

1. **Track Progress**
   - o "Use tools like action item logs and progress trackers to evaluate whether goals are being met. Regularly review outcomes to ensure alignment with organizational objectives."

2. **Encourage Reflection**
   - o "Ask your team: Did we meet our goals? What could we do better next time? Feedback fosters continuous improvement."

3. **Celebrate Achievements**
   - o "Recognize contributions, big or small. Whether through verbal praise or formal acknowledgments, celebrating success builds morale and reinforces accountability."

At her next meeting, Maya put Alex's advice into action. She began by clearly outlining the meeting's purpose: to finalize and align the marketing strategy with company goals.

Throughout the discussion, Maya encouraged input from everyone, ensuring even the quieter voices were heard. As the meeting wrapped up, she revisited the goals, summarized critical decisions, and assigned follow-ups with deadlines. Before the team left, she acknowledged their collective effort.

"That felt different," Maya thought as the team dispersed. This wasn't just another meeting but a step forward, guided by intention and purpose.

Alex left Maya with these takeaways:

- How do my personal meeting goals align with my team's needs and organizational objectives?
- What steps can I take to ensure accountability and follow-through on meeting goals?
- How can I celebrate success to motivate my team and reinforce positive behaviors?

Leaders can transform meetings into purposeful, productive experiences that drive meaningful results by setting clear goals, fostering accountability, and reflecting on outcomes.

Conclusion: The Journey Beyond Meetings

Meeting Mastery Journal

Maya leaned back in her chair, a sense of clarity and purpose washing over her. The shift she felt wasn't just about running better meetings but about stepping into her potential as a leader. She realized meetings were not just about getting things done but creating a space for alignment, collaboration, and growth.

Like Maya, you've explored the strategies, mindsets, and tools that transform meetings from mundane obligations into meaningful, results-driven conversations. Each chapter of this book has been a step toward empowering you to lead with clarity, purpose, and intention. But as every great leader knows, the work doesn't stop here.

Mastering meetings is an ongoing process that thrives

on reflection, refinement, and accountability. To truly embrace this journey, you need a companion to help you put these insights into practice. That's where the *Meeting Mastery Journal* comes in.

Introducing the *Meeting Mastery Journal*

The *Meeting Mastery Journal* is designed to take the lessons from this book and turn them into action. It's a tool to help you bridge the gap between theory and practice, guiding you to:

- **Prepare with Purpose**: Craft thoughtful meeting objectives, align participants, and set the stage for meaningful outcomes.

- **Reflect with Intention**: Evaluate what worked, what didn't, and where you can grow as a leader.

- **Track Your Growth**: Document your progress, celebrate achievements, and refine your approach to foster a culture of accountability.

Whether you're preparing for a high-stakes strategy session or debriefing a weekly team meeting, the *Meeting Mastery Journal* provides a structured space to sharpen your skills and deepen your impact.

As you step away from this book and back into your leadership role, remember this: great meetings reflect great leadership. They're a mirror of your ability to inspire, align, and empower those around you. By using the *Meeting Mastery Journal*, you'll not only elevate the quality of your meetings but also grow into a more intentional and impactful leader.

The journey doesn't end here—it evolves with every

decision you make and every meeting you lead. Pick up your journal and take the next step toward mastering meetings and unlocking your leadership potential. Your team, your organization, and your future self will thank you.

Let's reimagine meetings together, one purposeful conversation at a time.

About the Author

Brenda Dixon is a passionate leadership coach, organizational consultant, and author dedicated to helping individuals and teams unlock their potential.

As the founder of Udugu Journey LLC, a coaching and consulting firm inspired by the Swahili concept of interconnectedness, Brenda empowers leaders to create inclusive environments that inspire collaboration and growth. Her unique approach blends practical strategies with a deep understanding of people, culture, and team dynamics.

When not coaching or writing, Brenda enjoys life on her farm in Stafford, Virginia, with her husband, children, and beloved dogs. She's committed to building strong communities and inspiring meaningful connections.